Printed by IngramSpark

First Printing, 2019

ISBN 978-17-09989-43-8

This research has been supported by NSF grants:

#HRD-1137483

#DRL-1420036

www.tiltfactor.com

CUTTING THROUGH THE BIAS:

USING GAMES AND INTERACTIVE EXPERIENCES TO TRANSFORM BIAS AGAINST WOMEN IN STEM

Table of Contents

Background

In 2014, an interdisciplinary group of researchers at Dartmouth College, University at Buffalo, and Carnegie Mellon University came together to combat gender disparity in the sciences. Together these three principal investigators began the Interactive Narrative Technology to Reduce Implicit Negative Stereotyping and Improve the Climate in STEM for Underrepresented Students (INTRINSICS) project. They set out to accomplish this goal by designing interactive experiences and leveraging breakthrough technology to support the development of and combat biases against women in the science, technology, engineering, and math (STEM) fields.

The need for greater representation of women and people from diverse racial and ethnic groups and lower socioeconomic strata in STEM courses, majors, and careers in the United States is indisputable. Women constitute 46.5% of the US workforce, yet they hold just 25% of all math and computer science jobs and 11% of engineering jobs.[1] Women in these fields often face pervasive stereotypes

[1] U.S. Department of Labor, Bureau of Labor Statistics (2009). Women in the labor force: A databook (Report 1018). Washington, DC: U.S. Department of Labor.

[2] https://nsf.gov/statistics/2016/nsb20161/#/

[3] Babeo, E., & Ellis, R. (2007). Four decades of STEM degrees, 1966-2004: The devil is in the details. STEM Workforce Data Project: Report No. 6. Washington, DC: Commission on Professionals in Science and Technology.

[4] Pascarella, E. T., Hagedorn, L. S., Whitt, E. J., Yeager, P. M., Edison, M. I., Terenzini, P. T., & Nora, A. (1997). Women's perceptions of a" chilly climate" and their cognitive outcomes during the first year of college. Journal of College Student Development, 38, 109-24.

that can hinder their ability to succeed. As a result, they comprise less than 30% of the science and engineering workforce in the U.S.[2] The numbers for racial minority groups and those from lower socio-economic groups are similarly sobering; for example, according to recent statistics, African Americans and Hispanics held only 6.2% and 5.3% of all STEM positions respectively.[3]

Social and psychological factors, in particular the prevalence and persistence of negative stereotypes toward underrepresented group members' abilities in STEM, play a key role in explaining — and perpetuating — this imbalanced level of participation in STEM. In particular, the prevalence and persistence of subtle "micro-inequalities" caused by implicit biases and stereotypes (which have taken the place of more overt, intentional forms of discrimination) have contributed to the "chilly climate" faced by underrepresented groups in STEM classrooms.[4]

The INTRINSICS Team

Dr. Mary Flanagan is the founder of the Tiltfactor game design and research lab at Dartmouth College. Since 1999, Dr. Flanagan has created video games to combat real-world inequality, such as The Adventures of Josie True and RAPUN-SEL which teach vital computer skills to young women and other underrepresented groups in STEM.

At Tiltfactor, Dr. Flanagan leads a team that develops game interventions using a unique strategy called Embedded Design. Unlike typical interventions for social change in which a purpose is explicitly stated, Embedded Design uses a sleight-of-hand: creators hide the game's true purpose within the broader context of the player's experience. As a result, Tiltfactor games do not seem like interventions on the surface. In controlled studies, researchers have demonstrated that this groundbreaking strategy increases the efficacy of prosocial interventions and makes players more likely to engage in the project, and play Tiltfactor games again and again.[5]

Dr. Melanie Green brings together communication and social psychological research to highlight the power of narratives in her lab at the University at Buffalo. Dr. Green's expertise in narrative transportation — an approach that, through stories, "transports" readers into the minds and experiences of others — allows the INTRINSICS team to increase empathy and motivate change with the power of story. Like games, stories can be subtle but effective methods of changing beliefs while keeping students engaged.

Dr. Geoff Kaufman heads the eheart (Enhancing Human Experiences, Attitudes, and Relationships with Technology) lab in the Human-Computer Interaction Institute at Carnegie Mellon University. He and his students study the transformative impact of interaction technologies, games, and storytelling platforms that aim to enhance personal expression and improve social dynamics. Their cross-disciplinary approach blends theories and methods from psychology, design, and computer science, to create and study new technologies and systems for social impact.

[5] Flanagan, M., & Kaufman, G. (2016). Shifting implicit biases with games using psychology: The embedded design approach. In Y. Kafai, G. Coleman, & B. Tynes (Eds.), Diversifying Barbie and Mortal Kombat: Intersectional Perspectives and Inclusive Designs in Gaming. Pittsburgh: CMU/ETC Press.

The Tiltfactor Team during the spring of 2018

Core Research Team:

Dr. Gili Freedman

Max Seidman

Sukdith Punjashtitkul

Danielle Taylor

Spring Yu

Gareth Solbeck

Kaitlin Fitzgerald

Student Team

Rachel Billings

Perrin Brown

Elinor Dooley

Grace Dorgan

Sarah Drescher

Nicholas Feffer

Catalina Garcia

Rijul Garg

Jonathan Gliboff

Jordan Hall

Rachel Hand

Bineshii Hermes-Roach

Amanda Herz

Emma Hobday

Julia Holgado

Sara Holston

Zuff Idries

Ruba Iqbal

Jiachen Jiang

Khevna Joshi

James Kehoe

Jaclyn Kimball

Lindsay Kusnarowis

Catilyn Lee

Savannah Liu

Abigail Livingston

Patrick Matlin Redondo

LeJohn Montgomery

Melissa Moore

Jesus Moreno

Sophie Neumann

Amina Ospan

Elaine Paravati

Mikaela Schulz

Andrea Sedlacek

Nicole Sellew

Sarah Senkfor

Eun Ji Seo

Nikita Shaiva

Luisa Vasquez

Alexis Wallace

Amanda Young

Special Thanks To

Farooq Ahmed

Naomi Clark

Nomi Kane

Alannah Linkhorn

Charlie Laud

Producto Studios

SuperGenius Studio

What's the Problem?

Research continues to reveal that biases persist in STEM education contexts, even among individuals who value fairness and, moreover, even among professionals who are themselves members of underrepresented groups. These biases occur on the part of both educators[6] and students,[7] subtly but powerfully affecting their perceptions, expectations, and behaviors toward learners from underrepresented groups. As a result, instructors are often not fully cognizant of the ways that their own classroom practices may unintentionally threaten the self-esteem and confidence of underrepresented group members. At the same time, students who belong to stereotyped groups often feel reluctant or powerless to express their experiences of bias openly for fear of judgment or rebuke.[8] This combination of factors perpetuates the chilly classroom climate in STEM and has been shown to have a direct influence on the decision of women, minorities — and even, in some cases, white, male students — to opt against or leave STEM majors and careers.[9]

Given the subtlety of both the expression and the effects of most "modern" forms of bias,[10] and the proven, direct impact of bias on attrition rates in STEM, there is an urgent need to provide those involved in STEM classrooms with greater awareness of implicit bias and its deleterious influence. Our team's aim of developing novel and effective ways to improve classroom climate is particularly imperative for those STEM areas with the highest levels of persistent imbalances in representation.

[6] Isbell, L. A., Young, T. P., & Harcourt, A. H. (2012). Stag parties linger: continued gender bias in a female-rich scientific discipline. PloS one, 7, e49682

[7] Anderson, K. J. (2010). Students' stereotypes of professors: An exploration of the double violations of ethnicity and gender. Social Psychology of Education, 13, 459-472.

[8] Tatum, H. E., Schwartz, B. M., Schimmoeller, P. A., & Perry, N. (2013). Classroom participation and student-faculty interactions: Does gender matter? The Journal of Higher Education, 84, 745-768.

[9] Beasley, M. A., & Fischer, M. J. (2012). Why they leave: The impact of stereotype threat on the attrition of women and minorities from science, math and engineering majors. Social Psychology of Education, 15, 427-448.

[10] Dovidio, J. F., & Gaertner, S. L. (2004). Aversive racism. Advances in Experimental Social Psychology, 36, 1-52.

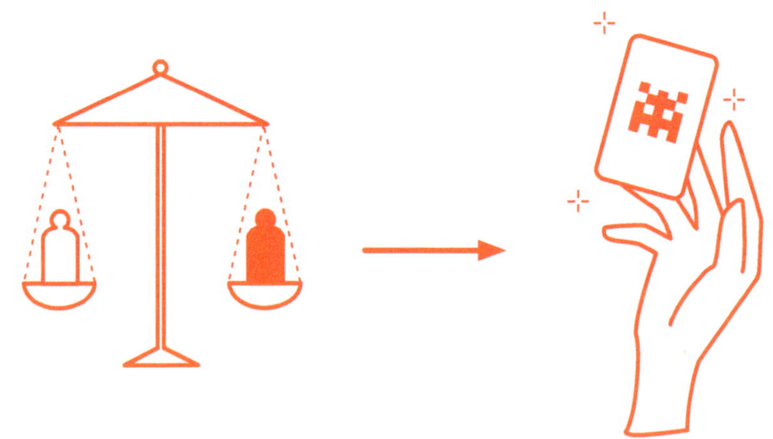

This book focuses on the development, assessment, and deployment of our set of digital interactive narrative interventions, called IN-TRINSICS (Interactive Narrative Technology for Reducing Implicit Negative Stereotyping and Improving the Climate in STEM), for use by introductory-level undergraduate STEM instructors and their students. The INTRINSICS interventions serve a fourfold purpose:

1 Provide students, particularly students from underrepresented groups (e.g., women and racial/ethnic minorities), a safe, accessible arena in which to express their subjective classroom experiences of stereotype threat, bias, and perceived inequity

2 Give instructors and students alike the opportunity to gain greater insights about underrepresented students' unique subjective experiences and psychological perspectives in STEM

3 Present instructors themselves with a "mirror" on their own behavioral and instructional practices, particularly those that may be affected by implicit bias

4 Ultimately empower instructors and students alike to be more aware, vigilant, and proactive in responding to the experiences of institutional-level or personal-level discrimination perceived and experienced by underrepresented students

The INTRINSICS team applies design thinking to create narratives, games, mobile apps, and other interventions to bolster women's sense of belonging and decrease their self-doubt in STEM. Our work also confronts stereotypes about women in STEM to decrease all participants' negative perceptions.

The INTRINSICS team builds on the work of social psychologists who have studied implicit bias and stereotypes. Our interventions seek to address the so-called "micro-inequalities" that have taken the place of more overt, intentional forms of discrimination and have contributed to the underrepresentation of women and minorities in STEM classrooms and careers. Our work demonstrates that novel interventions such as games can change cultural stereotypes and thus can play a central role in increasing both the size and diversity of the STEM talent pool. Our research is of great practical significance to educators, designers, psychologists, and anyone concerned about the next generation of America's science and engineering leadership.

Embedded Design

A set of principles that ensures both a player's engagement with a game and the effectiveness of the intervention is maximized.

Many of our interventions are informed by Tiltfactor's **Embedded Design** model. Embedded Design is a set of principles that ensures both a player's engagement with a game and the effectiveness of the intervention is maximized. Typical prosocial interventions often broadcast their intentions, which can lead participants to react against them — nullifying the attempt.

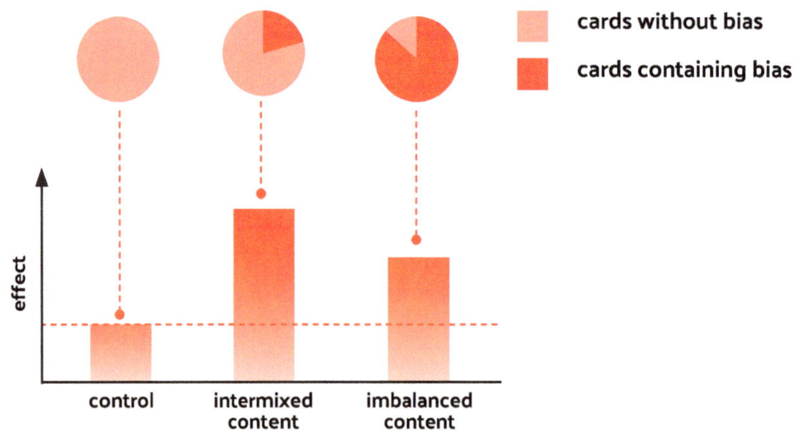

Less is more: Tiltfactor used the Embedded Design strategy to help the card game **Awkward Moment** fight bias. The game showed less effect when 90% of the cards contained some element of bias.

The Embedded Design approach changes players' attitudes in three ways:

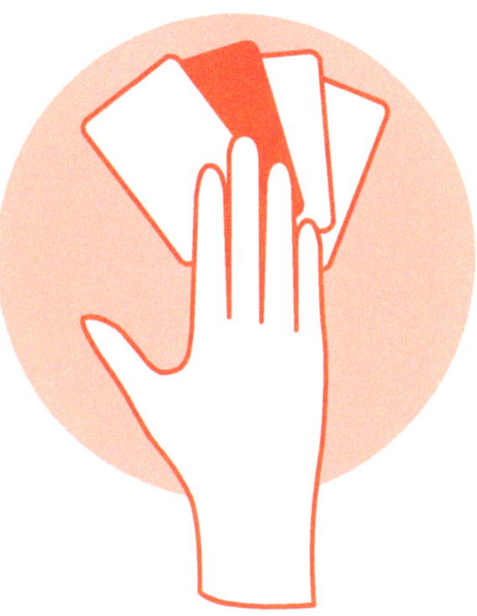

Intermixing on-message and off-message content

Obfuscating its true persuasive aims

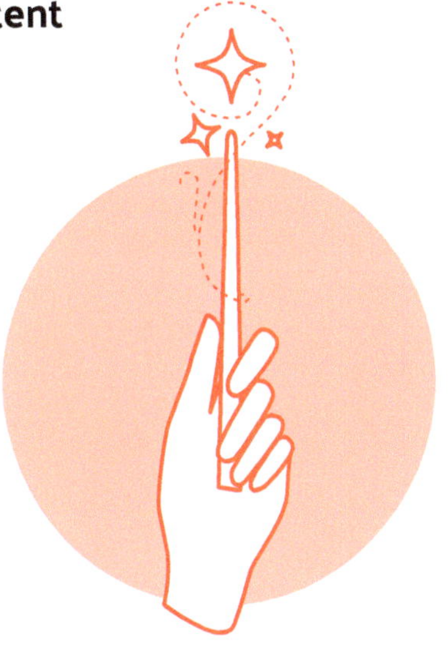

Distancing players from real-life situations and their own identities, preconceptions, and beliefs

Our Work

The INTRINSIC team's recent work, supported by the National Science Foundation's Research on Education and Learning (REAL) program,[11] develops and deploys a set of interactive digital interventions that:

- provides underrepresented students a safe and accessible arena in which to express their classroom experiences;

- gives instructors and students the opportunity to gain greater insights about underrepresented students' unique experiences;

- presents instructors with a "mirror" of their own behavioral and instructional practices;

- and empowers instructors and students alike to be proactive in responding to the experiences of underrepresented students.

Our many thoughtfully-crafted interventions give students the power to infuse their own real-life experiences into the projects. As a result, these interventions have the potential to improve the STEM classroom climate for all learners.

[11] https://www.nsf.gov/pubs/2013/nsf13604/nsf13604.htm

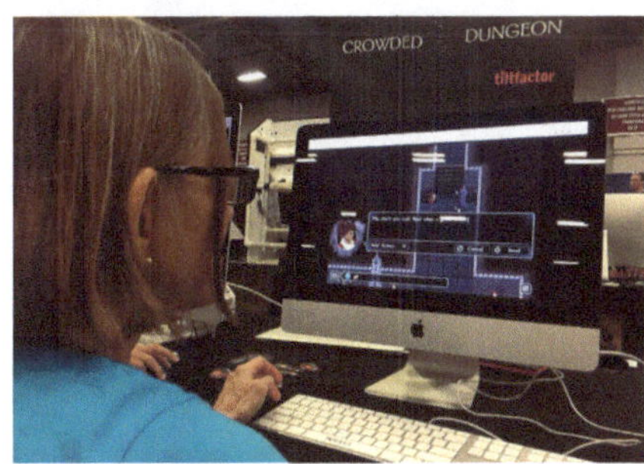

Narratives that Encourage Identification with Women in STEM

Stories are immensely powerful tools for immersing readers in new and unfamiliar worlds; they can transport individuals into different points of view and give them experiences they would otherwise never have had access to. **Can stories help men and women identify more with women facing challenges in STEM?** Will certain points of view be more credible than others? And what about whether someone thinks a story is fictional, like a film or a book, versus a situation that is more documentary in nature?

In our research on the power of narratives in science, in order to develop interactive systems and games to shift the dynamic of women in STEM, we confronted holes in the literature about the impact of stories and narrative point of view, and found that we needed to do some fundamental research. Research has shown that small but important details in the way narratives are crafted can lead to different outcomes. For example, first-person voice can be more effective at encouraging readers to adopt the mind-set of a character they are reading about than other narrative voices.[12] First-person voice facilitates a sense of immediacy and connection to the character, while the third-person voice encourages a more passive observer-perspective.

Students received significant benefits from reading fictional narratives written in first-person narration.

We created stories that allow people to experience the world through the eyes of a woman in STEM. This intervention strategy represents a novel way to engage participants with unfamiliar realms — or see familiar ones in new ways!

The interactive and traditional narratives we wrote depicted "Trisha," a first-year college student who intends to major in physics, and her experience of anxiety and self-doubt in her introductory university STEM class. We invited over 400 students to read the narratives, in order to answer the question: how might reading stories about Trisha impact readers' attitudes towards underrepresented groups in STEM?

[12] Kaufman, G. and Libby, L. Changing Beliefs and Behavior Through Experience-Taking *Journal of Personality and Social Psychology*, March 26, 2012.

Professor Donaldson specifically asked about the ballistic trajectory problem I'd aced on the last homework assignment.

"Well done, Trisha. Very few students were able to come up with that solution. I was very impressed. Just out of curiosity, did you do all the calculations yourself, or did you have some help?"

My first thought was to erupt with anger, but I bit my tongue and instead said calmly, "No, that was all my work, professor, but thank you"

Stereotype Threat

The finding that merely being reminded of a stereotype about oneself can negatively impact one's performance.

Versions of Trisha's story included events (like the above excerpt) known to trigger "**stereotype threat**" — the finding that merely being reminded of a stereotype about oneself can negatively impact one's performance. We then studied the impact of two key variables on stereotype threat. The first variable was the use of first-person ("I", "me"), second-person ("you"), or third-person ("she") narrative voice in the story. The second variable was the framing of the narrative as either fictional or autobiographical.

In our study of the versions of the narrative, we found significant benefits for college students when they read first-person narration, and also, a bit surprisingly, when students were told the story they were reading was fictional.

The students who read these narratives felt more transported into the story and more closely identified with the storyteller — the fictional female STEM student. These first-person, fictionalized narratives also led to an increased awareness of bias compared to second- and third-person accounts of her experiences that used a biographical framing.

Finally, we found that male student participants were less likely than female participants to attribute the female storyteller's anxiety to bias-related factors, such as an awareness of stereotypes or instructor's treatment. Instead, male participants were more likely to attribute the anxiety to the character's lack of preparation.[13]

[13] Freedman, G., Fitzgerald, K., Green, M. C., Kaufman, G., Flanagan, M. (November, 2017). Using narratives to raise awareness of stereotype threat in STEM. Paper presented at the 2017 Annual Conference of the National Communication Association, Dallas, TX.

Why It Matters

These results are provocative because they fundamentally change the way educators should think about telling stories that reduce bias. It's often assumed that true stories will be more transformative than fictional tales. Rather than "tell the true story" of a female student struggling in STEM, our research shows that telling fictional stories may better help readers empathize with the experiences of women in STEM.

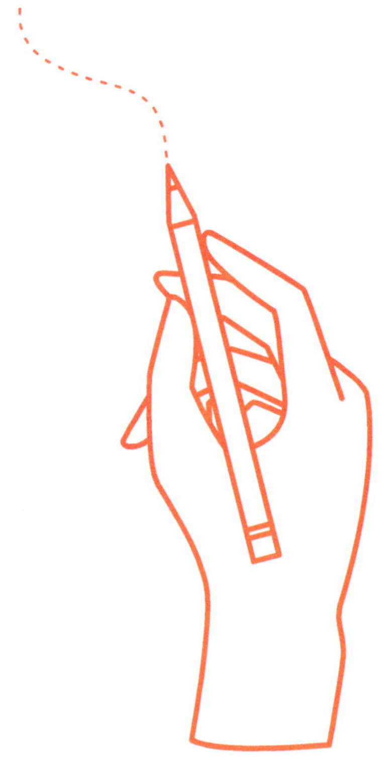

Personality Matters:
Writing about Experiences with Bias

Writing, such as journaling or keeping a diary, is often thought to be cathartic. Psychologists have found that writing about negative events, for example, can be good for both our mental and physical health. As we engaged with the power of storytelling, we decided to take a deeper look at this phenomenon and asked: **is writing about bias cathartic for everyone? Are there boundary conditions to the emotional benefits of expressive writing?** Are some personality traits associated with benefiting more or less from writing about negative experiences? We focused on the experience of being the target of stereotypical or biased judgments — a type of event which has received little attention in prior research.

One size does not fit all when it comes to writing about negative experiences; not all students found writing about bias to be cathartic.

To understand the role that personality plays, we asked over 200 college students to write about a time when they had been the target of bias or prejudice. We were motivated by the concern that some personalities might process or react differently toward writing as an act of reflection and healing.

Our study found that these writing exercises had different effects on different types of people. Individuals with high self-esteem were protected from feeling negative emotions when writing about experiences with biases. However, those who were concerned with how others perceive them (i.e., had higher levels of public self-consciousness) were more likely to experience negative emotions when writing about biases.[14]

[14] Green, M. C., Kaufman, G., Flanagan, M., & Fitzgerald, K. (2017). Self-esteem and public self-consciousness moderate the emotional impact of expressive writing about experiences with bias. Personality and Individual Differences, 116, 212–215. http://doi.org/10.1016/j.paid.2017.04.057

Why It Matters

Our work demonstrates that one size does not fit all when it comes to writing interventions: educators must consider the role that personality plays when eliciting narratives so as to first 'do no harm.' This research has dramatic implications for the development of interventions to help individuals overcome trauma, bias, and prejudice.

Decreasing Self-Doubt among Women in STEM

Many of the challenges facing women in STEM are made worse by a pervasive sense of self-doubt. **Can a game act as a defense against these internalized feelings of doubt?** We set out to discover whether this was possible.

In our digital, point-and-click adventure puzzle game, **The Enchanter**, we use Embedded Design strategies to help female undergraduate STEM students actively **restructure** the biases and self-doubt they may feel. The game aims to provide a setting in which students can silence negative thoughts and focus on overcoming obstacles by externalizing their negative self-talk (e.g., "maybe they are right, and I'm not smart enough.")

Playing The Enchanter game decreased self-doubt among women in introductory STEM courses.

In **The Enchanter**, players take on the role of a potion-making character named Gertie who has become a key figure in a fictional world. As she makes her way to her research lab, she encounters a range of gender-related obstacles that she must overcome. For example, an authority figure will not let her enter the lab because he is expecting the head alchemist to be a man — not a woman. Throughout the game, even the narrator expresses doubt about Gertie's abilities. To progress in the game, players must fight back again these multiple layers of doubt.

To test the effectiveness of this game on women's atti-

Different potions players can make

Your cauldron contains a *boiling sticky-sweet, milky, golden* concoction.

The potion-brewing screen in **The Enchanter**

tudes, we studied students' self-doubt over time. Our team recruited more than 200 female undergraduate students in introductory STEM courses. Each participant completed a questionnaire about self-doubt on day 1, played the game, completed the same questionnaire again on day 8, and then completed the questionnaire one last time on day 15.

We found that playing just one session of **The Enchanter** decreased self-doubt immediately and that players maintained this feeling for at least a week after.[15]

[15] Freedman, G., Seidman, M., Flanagan, M., Green, M. C., & Kaufman, G. (in prep). Using a game intervention to decrease self-doubt among female undergraduate STEM students.

Why It Matters

These results are provocative because fantastical games are often thought to have little real world impacts. Our findings act as proof that aspiring women scientists can overcome real world self-doubt by practicing reacting against negative self-talk, and that games can be a powerful tool to help them do so.

Challenging Biases about Women in STEM

Can suddenly realizing how your own prejudices affect your judgment in problem solving through an "aha" moment help you address your internalized biases?

Confronting one's own biases is a necessary act, but can leave students feeling defensive.

With our mystery puzzle game **The Investigation**, we set out to see whether these "aha" moments might help individuals confront the assumptions they unknowingly carry.

To test our hypothesis, we designed a study where students had to work in teams to deduce which character from a set of suspects might have stolen a biohazardous sample from a fictional university laboratory. Our team designed a mystery game for the study that required players to be open-minded about the gender of scientists and STEM researchers.

To help them solve the mystery, students received a packet of information pertaining to the case. Players tried to solve the puzzle using the information provided to them in the documents. The key to solving the mystery was to realize that one of the scientists was never explicitly gendered in the game. Realizing that this character is a woman (since almost all players assumed the character was a man) is **The Investgations**'s "aha" moment.

We conducted two studies, the first with 144 college students and the second with 374 high school students, to test whether this "aha" moment in **The Investigation** could decrease explicit biases towards women in STEM.

We found that high school students who played the game were significantly less likely to misgender scientist characters as men (compared to the students who played a control

The Investigation in its paper puzzle game form

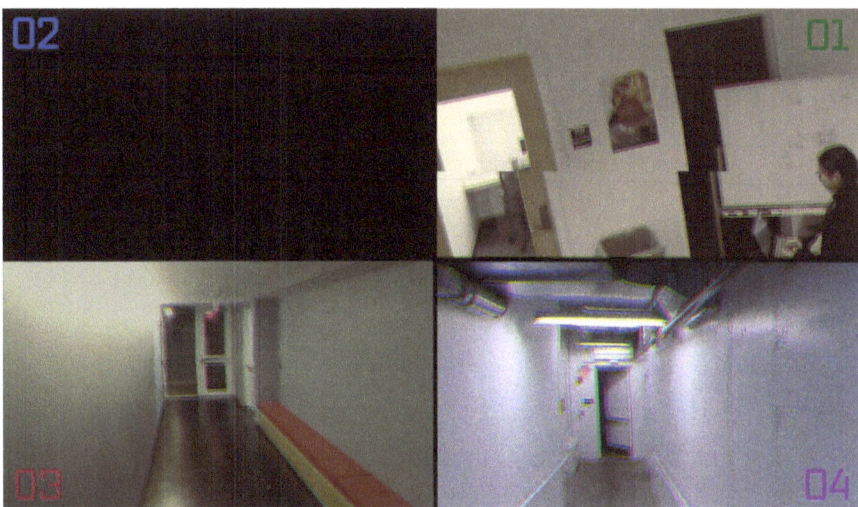

Security camera footage of the science building in the digital version of **The Investigation**

[16] Freedman, G., Seidman, M., Flanagan, M., Kaufman, G., & Green, M. C. (2018) The impact of an "aha" moment on gender biases: Limited evidence for the efficacy of a game intervention that challenges gender assumptions. *Journal of Experimental Social Psychology*, 78. doi: 10.1016/j.jesp.2018.03.014

condition of the game).[16] Interestingly, however, the students who played the game reported less positive views of women in science. In other words, being confronted with their own biases made the students act more carefully to counteract their implicit biases (by not misgendering the characters in the game), but caused the students to say that they were less open to women in science, possibly due to feeling defensive after playing. In addition, college students misgendered the scientists more than the high school students, and did not see any improvement after playing the game.

To increase the reach of this intervention, we also created an online version of **The Investigation** in which players scrolled through security camera footage to determine who stole the biohazardous sample from the lab, instead of reading interrogation transcripts. A preliminary study has shown the digital version of **The Investigation** reduced male students' biases, in the form of less prejudice against men choosing nursing careers.

Why It Matters

By forcing students to confront their own biases through an "aha" moment, we were able to get them to double check their assumptions about scientists and gender. Educators can use this strategy to decrease students' implicit biases – but they should be aware that confronting one's own biases is never easy, and students may feel defensive immediately after the intervention. Additionally, **The Investigation** shows that some societal biases may be too entrenched to change by the time students enter college. It is crucial that educators understand that certain types of interventions must be conducted before students leave secondary school.

Teaching Others the Tools We Use

Creating a game can be a daunting task, which explains why traditional media has been researched far more than games. To help other researchers create and study their own games and interactive narratives, our team published two papers detailing how we created **The Enchanter** and the interventions we used to study narrative voice and fictional framing.

The first paper describes how to use Twine, a tool for building interactive narratives, for psychological experiments.[17] We detail three distinct experimental paradigms that can benefit from a more interactive method, which Twine provides.

The second review article describes how games have been used in personality and social psychology in the past, how they can be used moving forward, and how to create a game specifically for research.[18]

[17] Freedman, G., Seidman, M., Flanagan, M., Kaufman, G., & Green, M. C. (2018). Updating a classic: A new generation of vignette experiments involving iterative decision-making. *Advances in Methods and Practices in Psychological Science.* doi: 10.1177/2515245917742982

[18] Freedman, G., & Flanagan, M. (2017). From dictators to avatars: Furthering social and personality psychology through game methods. *Social and Personality Psychology Compass, 11:* e12368. doi: 10.1111/spc3.12368

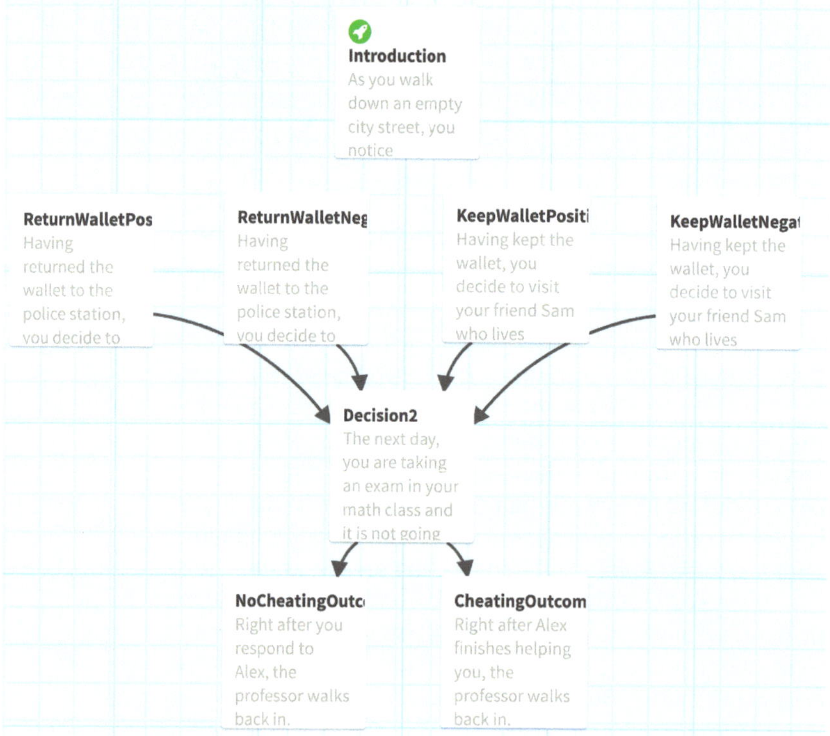

Layout of the vignette example Twine story shown in the "Updating a Classic" paper

Why It Matters

Researchers can use the methods and tools we describe to quickly and easily create game-driven studies. Our methodology will help the body of game research catch up to that of traditional forms of media.

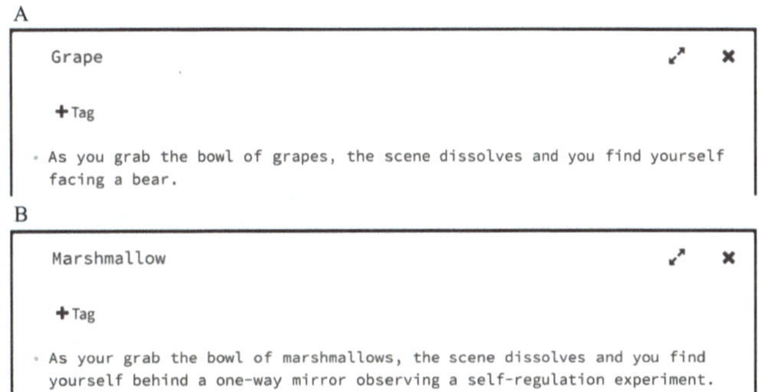

Twine story passage editor shown in the "Updating a Classic" paper

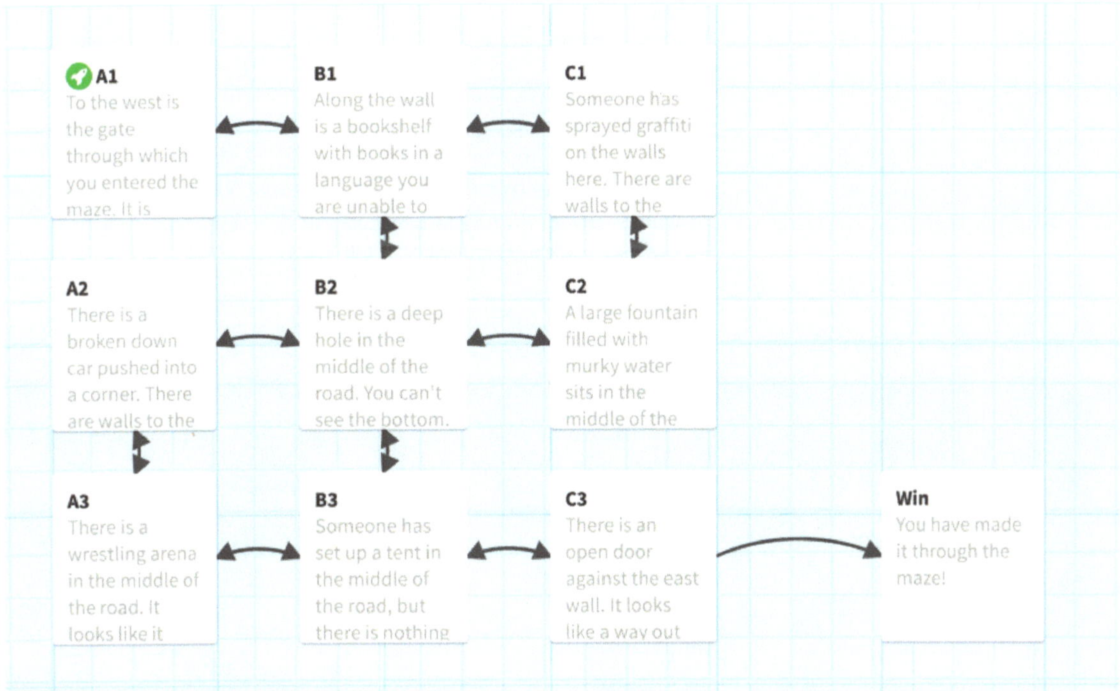

Layout of the maze example Twine story shown in the "Updating a Classic" paper

I Am More Than

Can we come together in a conversation about biases in STEM, and can we empower disadvantaged students in STEM by sharing stories of bias? To tap into university students' lived experiences in the sciences, we collected stories about the multiple ways students interact and live in their world.

Microaggression

A small action (usually a statement made in passing) that discriminates against or diminishes a member of a marginalized group. Microaggressions are often made unintentionally, but can have serious mental and physical effects on students over time.

We leveraged students' desire to share information online and created a website, **I Am More Than**, to provide them with a safe space to share stories about their experiences with bias, **microaggressions**, or stereotype threat. These stories could take many forms: experiences a person had, ones that someone witnessed, or observations of forces that perpetuate bias.

By allowing students to share stories, we illuminated the ways that prejudice can infiltrate everyday interactions, and we created a vivid representation of the multiple methods students use to traverse their emotional and physical landscapes.

Why It Matters

Microaggressions are an everyday occurrence for many people, and depicting those experiences can increase empathy for underrepresented groups in many fields, not just STEM. The image-based experiences that **I Am More Than** gathers can be widely shared online, giving it more reach than traditional interventions.

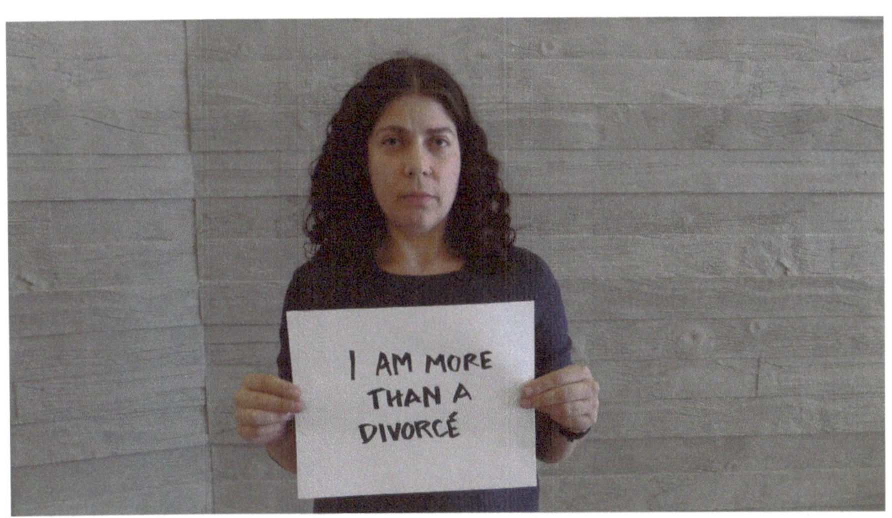

By collecting and sharing stories, we shed light on the deep and profound effect of stereotypes and prejudice.

I AM MORE THAN...

MICROAGGRESSION

-MICROASSAULT
-MICROINSULT
-MICROINVALIDATION

CAN AFFECT CONFIDENCE AND PERFORMANCE, AND ULTIMATELY LEAD PEOPLE TO SUCCUMB TO NEGATIVE STEREOTYPES

UNDER-REPORTED FORMS OF DISCRIMINATION

IMPLICIT BIAS

UNCONSIOUSLY COLORS OUR VIEWS AND ACTIONS WITH DOMINANT IDEAS (E.G., AFRICAN-AMERICANS ARE SUPERIOR ATHLETES, WHITE STUDENTS ARE SMARTER THAN BLACK STUDENTS, ASIANS ARE BETTER AT MATH)

STEREOTYPE THREAT

CAN CAUSE PEOPLE TO CONFORM TO NEGATIVE STEREOTYPES PLACED UPON THEM

WHY SHOULD I CARE?

PERFORMANCE

STEREOTYPE THREAT CAN DECREASE TEST SCORES, GRADES, ETC.

"I KNEW I WAS JUST AS INTELLIGENT AS EVERYONE ELSE... BUT FOR SOME REASON I DIDN'T SCORE WELL ON TESTS. MAYBE I WAS JUST NERVOUS. THERE'S A LOT OF PRESSURE ON YOU, KNOWING THAT IF YOU FAIL, YOU FAIL YOUR RACE."
STATE SENATOR
RODNEY ELLIS (D-TX)

WELLNESS

MICROAGGRESSIONS CAUSE:
-SELF-DOUBT
-ANXIETY
-FRUSTRATION
-SADNESS
-CONFUSION

"I KNEW WHAT THEY THOUGHT ABOUT BLACKS- THAT THEY WEREN'T SMART ENOUGH TO PLAY QUARTERBACK AND YOU COULD FEEL THEM BEING LESS PATIENT WITH MY MISTAKES THAN WITH THE OTHER GUYS."
WARREN MOON
8-TIME ALL-PRO NFL QUARTERBACK

ACHEIVEMENT

IMPLICIT BIAS MAKES PEOPLE FEEL LIKE THEY ARE NOT TAKEN SERIOUSLY AND FEAR THAT THEY DO NOT BELONG TO A PARTICULAR DOMAIN

"[AT PRINCETON] I FELT LIKE A VISITOR LANDING IN AN ALIEN COUNTRY. I HAVE SPENT MY YEARS SINCE PRINCETON, WHILE AT LAW SCHOOL, AND IN MY VARIOUS PROFESSIONAL JOBS, NOT FEELING COMPLETELY A PART OF THE WORLDS I INHABIT."
SONIA SOTOMAYOR
U.S. SUPREME COURT JUSTICE

WHY SHOULD I SHARE?

WE HAVE ALL FACED BIAS AND HAVE BEEN UNINTENTIONALLY BIASED

ENLIGHTEN OTHERS ABOUT YOUR EXPERIENCES

EMPOWER OTHERS TO SPEAK UP

ERADICATE BIAS

SHARE YOUR STORY @
HTTP://I-AM-MORE-THAN.ORG

Local Heroes: Campus Tours to Improve Representation of Women in STEM

Often, as we traverse familiar landscapes, we remain unaware of the history — both good and bad — that surrounds us. **Can hearing the history of those who have overcome challenges to succeed in STEM inspire students to do the same?** Building from University of Pennsylvania Professor Jonah Berger's work on the role of social influence, we created a Dartmouth campus tour to test whether learning about unknown local stories could generate "social currency" and inspire students to study science or to continue if they already were studying STEM.

The campus tour provides real instances of bias in STEM and tells of how individuals overcame those challenges.

Augmented Reality

Technology which overlays graphics over the real world. AR is used in advanced headsets and glasses, but can also work on smartphones using the camera functionality!

Instead of relying on the traditional campus tour with its trained tour guides and schedules, we built our own: a technologically advanced campus tour that uses a sophisticated, locative-media, **augmented reality**, mobile phone app to introduce new students to the Dartmouth College campus. Because of its self-guided locative technology, the tour can be taken by anyone with a smartphone at any time.

The tour features stories about former students, including those of students overcoming real instances of bias in STEM fields throughout the college's history. The app explains how the selected scientists featured in the tour overcame those challenges — thus informing students of relatable role models from the Dartmouth community.

A cast of recurring characters recount the stories, which are contextualized within a larger narrative about the campus. For example, a character named Chad describes how a men's-only medical fraternity at Dartmouth admitted a female student into their society in defiance of the national organization's mandate. Another story describes how a female physics student was crushed because she believed that she received the lowest score on a midterm exam in the class. The tour reveals how she eventually learned that

Why It Matters

The significance of this project lies in its unique approach to combating bias in STEM. By using cutting edge technology, the campus tour captures student interest. It then introduces participants to little known facts and traditions from campus history while mixing in bias-related STEM content. This novel approach demonstrates that embodying narratives into real and virtual space can craft influential role models and create local heroes.

many of the men in the class had done much worse. The app also highlights the accomplishments of recent Dartmouth graduates, including two female computer scientists who now work for companies such as Electronic Arts and Apple.

The INTRINSICS team further pushed technological boundaries to create a virtual reality (VR) version of this campus tour to provide an even more immersive experience for students that could be played indoors and even from off campus. As in the locative mobile app, students explored the campus and found stories about the—at times dark—history of the college. We then studied whether the app and VR version could improve the retention of more than 250 undergraduate women and underrepresented minorities in STEM. Preliminary results show that the VR version inspired STEM students and helped them believe that they could succeed in their science and engineering courses.

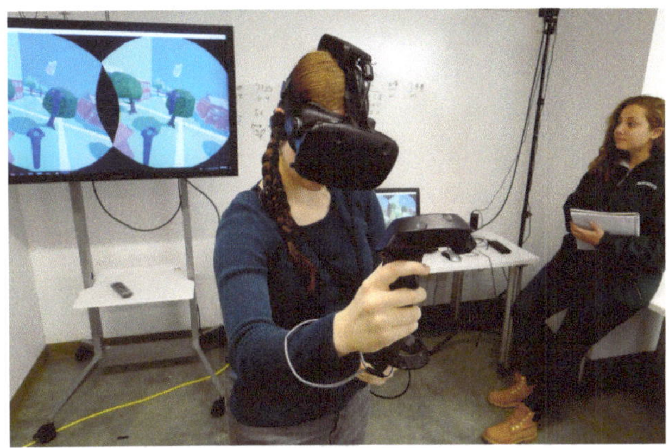

The technology behind the campus tour allows it to be transferred to other campuses. Campus leaders could generate their own campus tours by inserting stories and images from their own universities. Bias is a part of our society that every university has to grapple with, but where there are stories of bias, there will always be stories of individuals overcoming bias.

Crowdsourcing Responses to Bias

Can crowdsourcing be used to collect possible responses to situations of bias from real world players? Could students use a game to offer novel methods to combat prejudice if given the opportunity to do so?

Crowdsourcing

Collecting data by letting crowds on the internet contribute. Crowdsourcing has many applications, from identifying objects in a photograph to predicting what shape proteins will form into.

We created Crowded Dungeon, a partially text-based adventure game that uses player-written narratives.[19] The refrain of traditional text adventure games has always been "I don't understand your command"—the response when the game system has not been programmed to recognize what the player has typed. Unlike other text-based adventure games, which rely on a finite number of pre-scripted responses, Crowded Dungeon is freeform and dynamic: players can type anything they want, and the game AI responds with the best response it can come up with.

Crowded Dungeon investigates crowdsourcing in game design by inviting players to write anti-bias narratives.

Players can choose their role either as the hero trying to convince the monsters to let them pass, or as the monsters themselves. The game uses a crowdsourcing process to collect monster responses and then provides the hero with a seemingly infinite number of options for traversing the dungeon. Players in the monster role dictate the monsters' personalities as well as the strategies the hero can use to get past them.

Players taking on the role of the hero trying to get past Grumbles the troll might type phrases like:

- You look hungry. Let me pass if I give you a sandwich? #give [Poison Sandwich]

- Nice hair. I've got some oil to make it really shine. Can you let me pass? #give [Oily Residue]

- Hi! Can you let me through the door?

- Surprise! #attack

[19] http://www.tiltfactor.org/game/crowded-dungeon

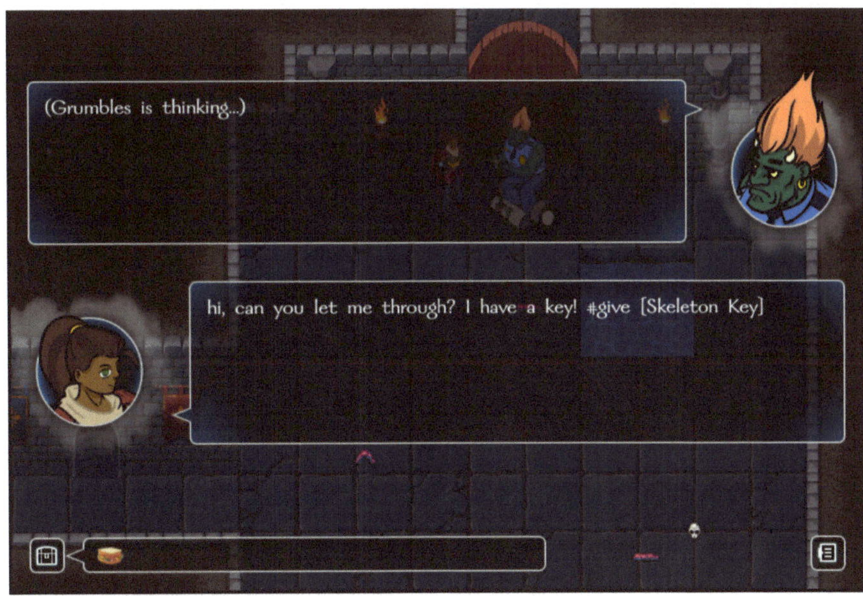

The hero waits for a response from Grumbles the troll in **Crowded Dungeon**

If a player is playing the role of Grumbles the troll, that player then writes a response and decides whether the hero deserves to continue. Once enough potential responses have been recorded, players no longer need to take on the role of Grumbles. Instead, the game system can choose the most appropriate response for Grumbles based on hundreds of responses that real players have typed for Grumbles in the past.

Why It Matters

Crowded Dungeon provides a rich collection of situations for players to respond to, including many settings in which bias could occur. To collect anti-bias responses, the game is built with the ability to simulate a computer-controlled hero and make her say scripted phrases.

These phrases can be used to set up situations of bias, and allow the human-controlled monster player to respond to the bias experiences, thus collecting a broad range of possible responses to microaggressions and other situations of bias. This work further contributes to our understanding of the specific ways that prejudice is enacted in our environments and institutions.

Addressing Prejudice Through Social Media and Comics

Brief amusing messages on social media have the potential to raise awareness about gender biases in STEM by reducing defensive reactions. Our team aimed to examine the differences in the way comics and text have the capacity to impact readers. **Can comics about bias encourage more empathy and less prejudice in their readers?**

To study the impact potential of comics, we recruited over 400 participants and either showed them a set of tweets discussing bias, or a set of tweets containing our bias-related comics that we commissioned.[20] The study centered on social media, images, comics, and stereotypes in science to see if comics are more effective at increasing awareness about the biases facing women in STEM than simple text media feeds.

[20] We worked with the Center for Cartoon Studies in White River Junction, Vermont and artist Naomi Kane for this part of the research.

We found that women, but not men, felt less defensive regarding their views about women in STEM after viewing either type of post. After reading either type of post, participants viewed the climate for women in STEM as less positive, since the posts reminded them of the presence of bias in STEM. However, women who saw the comics perceived STEM fields to be more gender-balanced after reading the comics, but men's perceptions did not change. Thus, the results provide evidence that comics about women in STEM may be effective at changing women's perceptions about women in STEM.

Additionally, the study revealed that people seemed more willing to share the text-only tweets, even though the comic tweets seemed more effective at shifting opinions. This reflects the common intervention problem that we repeatedly discuss in our work: creating interventions that are both enjoyable and effective.

Why It Matters

Popular culture media forms such as comics and tweets have the potential to shift opinions and sharing behaviors, and both reduced defensiveness about gender biases and increased understanding about the climate for women in STEM. However, only comics were effective at positively changing women's beliefs regarding the number of women in STEM. Importantly, the comics and tweets were most often effective with the women in the study, not the men.

With further research into this phenomenon, we hope to learn how to harness the powerful forms of comics and social media and turn them into empirically-validated instruments with which to confront bias.

How do Obituaries Affect Perceptions of Scientists?

Well-known scientists can inspire the general public to learn more about their field of study. But after they die? Obituaries are an understudied form of culture; in the wake of the death of well known physicist Stephen Hawking, who died on March 14, 2018, we asked: **could Dr. Steven Hawking's obituary impact public perceptions of physics, his illness (amyotrophic lateral sclerosis), and overall, gender in science?**

In the studies, we recruited over 250 people to examine the influence of physicist Stephen Hawking's death on public interest in science topics related to his work. We also examined whether the representation of male versus female physicists quoted in the obituary increased perceptions of gender equity in science.

Our first study showed that reading Hawking's obituary increased interest in both physics and Dr. Hawking's illness, but that the number of female physicists quoted about Hawking did not affect interest levels in women or men.[21]

Our second study showed that following Hawking's death, there was a marked increase in Wikipedia page views on related topics in his research area and his illness, showing the influence of obituaries on the public.

Why It Matters

The positive effects of exposure to scientist role models from underrepresented groups is well-known. Our obituary research suggests that effects of so-called "megastar" scientist, while positive for increasing interest in STEM generally, may eclipse the presence of other underrepresented potential role models. Educators creating interventions to increase retention in STEM, therefore, should make scientist role models from underrepresented groups the focal points of their interventions, and may want to avoid focusing on more recognizable "megastar" scientists from well represented backgrounds.

[21] Freedman, G., Green, M. C., Flanagan, M., & Kaufman, G. (2019). Obituaries can popularize science and health: Stephen Hawking and interest in cosmology and amyotrophic lateral sclerosis. *Psychology of Popular Media Culture.* Advance online publication. doi: 10.1037/ppm0000233

Embodying Women Scientists in Virtual Reality

Since traditional narratives written from the point of view of marginalized groups can have deep impacts on readers, **could embodying a woman scientist decrease men's prejudices against women in STEM?** As a capstone to the INTRINSICS project, our team created a virtual reality (VR) escape room puzzle game called **Entangled**. In **Entangled**, players take on the role of Dr. Alex Smith, a physicist in a science fiction world who can manipulate objects in multiple dimensions. The player must use their skills to travel through the same science lab but in many different dimensions, escaping pursuit by a shadowy enemy.

Playing as a woman scientist in VR helped undergraduate men view women scientists as more competent.

Players initially assume that Dr. Smith is a man, but during the game they are offered a chance to glance into a virtual mirror and see that their character is actually a woman. **Entangled** builds on the "aha" moment approach our team used in **The Investigation**, but adds a VR reveal into the mix. In addition, the Embedded Design approach suggested to our team that making the gender reveal of the character less of a focus in the game might

Dr. Smith's lab and inventions in **Entangled**

increase its impact and decrease defensiveness. To this end, **Entangled** simply allows players to see their character in passing without calling unnecessary attention to the character or her gender.

Dr. Kaufman's research on traditional narratives has shown that delayed reveals of outgroup membership (for example, learning that the main character of a story is a member of another race or gender than the reader) leads to higher levels of **experience-taking**.[22] To study **Entangled**, the INTRINSICS team recruited over 200 male undergraduate students. In the first study, building on Dr. Kaufman's research, participants played the prototype of **Entangled** in virtual reality and saw their virtual avatar (Dr. Smith) in a digital mirror either at the start or the end of the experience. In the second study, players played a longer version of the prototype, saw their avatar either at the start or the end, and their avatar was either a man or a woman.

While the studies found no impact of when the character's gender was revealed on bias towards women in STEM, they showed that playing as a woman scientist increased players' perceptions of the degree of overlap of competence-related traits between women and scientists—rating women and scientists as more alike. Thus **Entangled** demonstrated potential for decreasing biases against women in science. After playing as a woman scientist, however, players rated Dr. Smith herself less positively, perhaps reacting to the challenge of the puzzles in the game.

[22] Kaufman, G. F., & Libby, L. K. (2012). Changing beliefs and behavior through experience-taking. *Journal of Personality and Social Psychology, 103*(1), 1-19. doi: 10.1037/a0027525

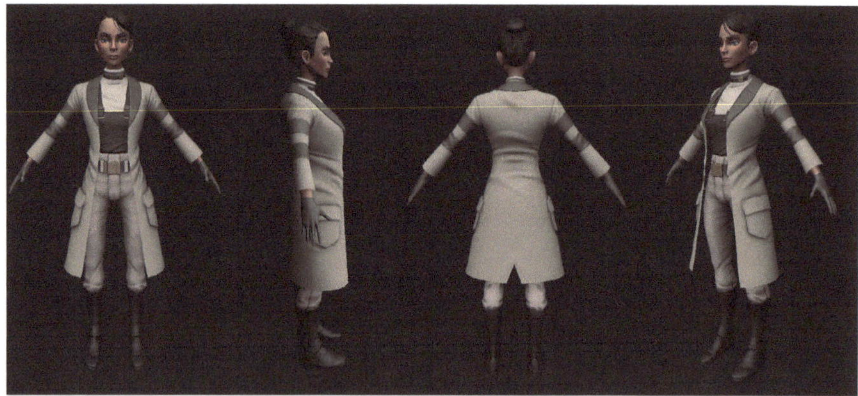

Turnaround for Dr. Smith's character model

Why It Matters

Research on **Entangled** showed that after playing as a woman scientist in VR, participants thought women and scientists were more alike in competence. **Entangled** demonstrates that virtual reality games have a profound potential to reduce bias (both within STEM, and in general) by allowing players to embody characters from marginalized groups.

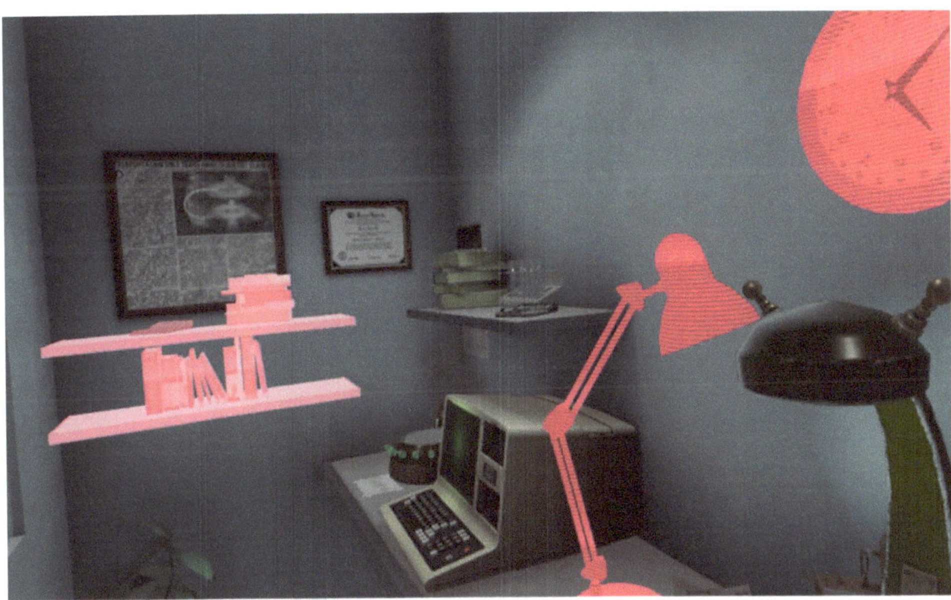

The red objects in Dr Smith's laboratory are from an adjacent universe to her own. The player cannot pick them up, and must work around them to solve puzzles.

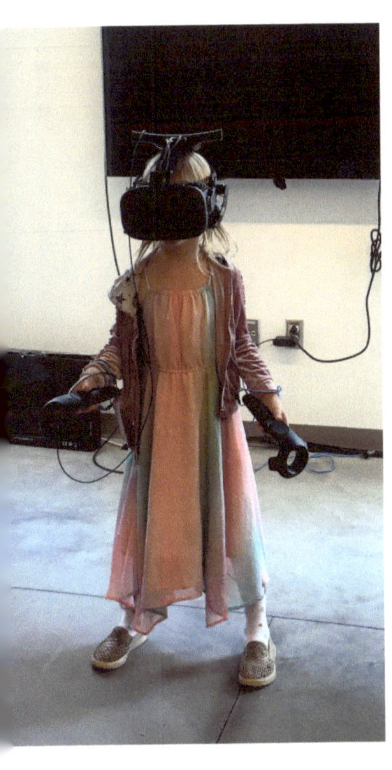

rep
buffalo
the name
dropping game

Foundational Work

Much of the INTRINSICS team's research was informed by a prior Tiltfactor project funded by the National Science Foundation's Early-Concept Grants for Exploratory Research (EAGER). With the support of EAGER, Tiltfactor demonstrated that purposefully designed games can change attitudes and beliefs about bias generally, and about women and girls in STEM specifically. In addition, Tiltfactor developed and verified the new design technique — Embedded Design — to accomplish this goal. We have spoken and published extensively on our games and on Embedded Design so that this work may have the broadest possible reach and impact.

In total, this project resulted in twenty game prototypes, seven of which were further developed and studied for the efficacy at reducing biases. Four of the games — **Awkward Moment, Awkward Moment at Work, Buffalo: the Name Dropping Game**, and **Luminaries** — produced statistically significant results against stereotype threat and implicit bias. The design of these games derives from psychological theories and research on stereotypes, cognition, and learning. Because games are an effective way of reaching those who might not otherwise be interested in confronting their biases, we believe this work continues to have a lasting impact far beyond traditional interventions.

Our studies with the games **Awkward Moment, Awkward Moment at Work**, and **Buffalo: the Name Dropping Game** have shown that the Embedded Design approach provokes a transformation in the game player and decreases implicit bias. Games overloaded with only anti-bias content have a reduced effect.[23] At the heart of our work is the notion that the replayability of fun and engaging games ensures their continuing effectiveness as interventions.

> **Professor Flanagan's team at Tiltfactor designed over twenty games to fight sexism in science, all of which informed the INTRINSICS team's work.**

[23] Kaufman, G., & Flanagan, M. (2015). A psychologically "embedded" approach to designing games for prosocial causes. Cyberpsychology: Journal of Psychosocial Research on Cyberspace, 9(3). http://doi.org/10.5817/CP2015-3-5

Awkward Moment

Can a card game confront biases about women in STEM? That's what we asked as we set out to design **Awkward Moment**. In order to do so, the game could not feel heavy-handed or players would tune out. We used our Embedded Design methodology and mixed on-topic and off-topic content to make an approachable, award-winning game with a satisfying play experience that secretly reworks players' biases.[24]

> **After playing Awkward Moment, kids were three times as likely to say that a scientist could be a woman.**

In the game, players draw Moment cards that put them in socially awkward situations with gender bias-related awkward moments mixed in. They take turns as the Decider and draw Reaction cards to impress the Decider by submitting the best reaction.

Using comprehensive social psychological measures, we conducted experiments to test the impact of **Awkward Moment**. We studied changes in players' likelihood of associating women with science, levels of assertiveness in responding to imagined occurrences of bias, and their perspective-taking abilities. Our results revealed that **Awkward Moment** exerts immediate positive effects for both young and old players![25]

[24] http://www.tiltfactor.org/game/awkward-moment

[25] Kaufman, G., & Flanagan, M. (2015). A psychologically "embedded" approach to designing games for prosocial causes. Cyberpsychology: Journal of Psychosocial Research on Cyberspace, 9(3). http://doi.org/10.5817/CP2015-3-5

Our study with **Awkward Moment** provided additional support for the efficacy of the Embedded Design strategy. The study investigated three ratios of bias to non-bias content to see which mixture was the most effective at impacting bias awareness and perception:

Neutral: No bias content

Intermixed: Less than 50% bias content

Overloaded: 90% bias content

Compared to participants in a neutral game condition, players of an 'intermixed' version of the game with less than half bias-related moments exhibited lower levels of prejudice and higher levels of perspective-taking. Of crucial importance, players of an 'overloaded' version of the game, with a majority of bias-related moments, exhibited **lower** levels of motivation to control prejudice and reduced perspective-taking than the intermixed game.

Why It Matters

The research with **Awkward Moment** demonstrates that well-designed games can be strategies to confront bias and increase perspective-taking. They can shift attitudes about women in science and inform game designers on the best ways to make effective games.

Awkward Moment at Work

Awkward Moment at Work[26] is the adult version of **Awkward Moment.** The game focuses on unfortunate workplace situations like accidental emails, wardrobe malfunctions, workplace romances — but moments related to gender bias are embedded within as in **Awkward Moment.**

Like **Awkward Moment**, **Awkward Moment at Work** is an engaging, repeatedly playable game that subtly changes players attitudes. This is significant because adults are not routinely exposed to anti-bias materials.

Why It Matters

Research on **Awkward Moment at Work** proves that the game serves as an effective intervention to promote women in STEM fields to the general public, without becoming a didactic form of diversity training.

After playing Awkward Moment at work, players showed less prejudice, and more easily took other people's perspectives.

Buffalo: the Name Dropping Game

Vast bodies of research have demonstrated that to counter stereotypes, people need to be exposed to examples that confront the stereotype.[27] Could a game get people to name examples of individuals who defy stereotypes, and thus help reduce bias?

Buffalo: the Name Dropping Game asks players to quickly think of famous historical, fictional, and pop-cultural figures, including politicians, scientists, artists, singers, and superheroes — intermixing underrepresented historical figures with well-known ones.[28] **Buffalo** is a party card game that can be equally enjoyed by both adults and families!

Our studies on **Buffalo** revealed that the game significantly lowered adult players' prejudices and increased their concern about being biased. We found that **Buffalo** was more effective at lowering prejudices when players were told that it was a game about "pop culture knowledge" than when they were told it was a game about "stereotypes".[29]

[27] McIntyre, R. B., Lord, C. G., Gresky, D. M., Ten Eyck, L. L., Frye, G. D. J., & Bond, C. F., Jr. (2005). A social impact trend in the effects of role models on alleviating women's mathematics stereotype threat. *Current Research in Social Psychology, 10*(9), 116–36.

[28] http://www.tiltfactor.org/game/buffalo

[29] Kaufman, G., & Flanagan, M. (2015). A psychologically "embedded" approach to designing games for prosocial causes. *Cyberpsychology: Journal of Psychosocial Research on Cyberspace, 9*(3), article 5.

The **Buffalo** Facilitator's Workbook by Kristen Toohill

Why It Matters

Through our studies we can conclude that **Buffalo** serves as an effective intervention to counter stereotypes and demonstrates one of the myriad ways in which games can reduce biases.

Luminists

Diverse scientists have existed throughout time and across the world — although many people remain unaware of them. Can a game help create awareness of global STEM role models? Could selecting role models from history speak to students from diverse backgrounds and increase student interest in STEM fields?

Our board game, **Luminists**, sought to answer those questions. The game transports players through the ages, introducing them to women and men who were history's greatest inventors, scientists, and engineers. Set in the year 2700 when society is unraveling from frivolous time travel, important scientific discoveries are slipping out of existence. Players must reinvent these discoveries by going back in time and enlisting the help of historical inventors. The winning player restores the most history by wisely recruiting luminists and making the most (re)discoveries.

A study on **Luminists** showed that the game effectively promoted players' interest in and perceived value of STEM careers — and specifically their interest in computer science. Once again, the Embedded Design method proved to be the determining factor for these outcomes: a version of the game with a balanced representation of men and women scientific role models (luminists) had a significantly greater impact than a version of the game where there were more women luminists than men.[30]

[30] Kaufman, G., Flanagan, M., & Seidman, M. (2015). Creating stealth game interventions for attitude and behavior change: An "embedded design" model. In Proceedings of DiGRA.

Why It Matters

Research using the **Luminists** game shows that games can broaden the minds and shift the attitudes of players towards greater inclusivity, simply by depicting diverse casts of competent characters.

Simply playing a game with a diverse cast of scientist characters increased kids' interest in STEM careers.

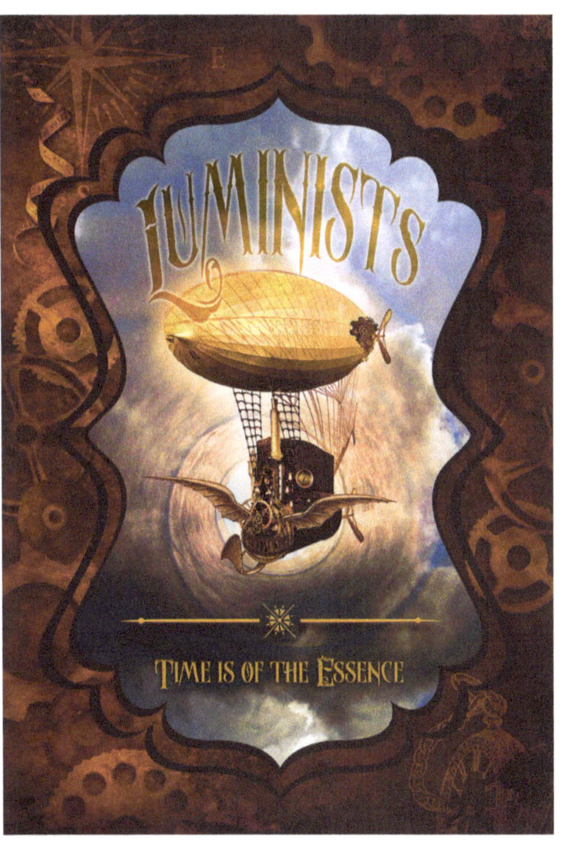

Selected Prototypes

Since Tiltfactor's inception in 2003, we have developed hundreds of game prototypes, some of which we refine further into interventions. A small sample of our game prototypes that combat biases and stereotypes are described below.

Moose Can't Jump

As mobile games have emerged as an international pastime, they present an exciting area in which to introduce anti-bias material. In the mobile game prototype **Moose Can't Jump**, players are introduced to stereotype threat in a novel, prosocial intervention. Participants plays as Melanie, a moose who has always believed that she can't jump or run as well as horses because she is a moose. Players help Melanie surmount the obstacles and overcome the stereotype threat triggered by other characters' insults. **Moose Can't Jump** both models stereotype threat and teaches players strategies for overcoming it.

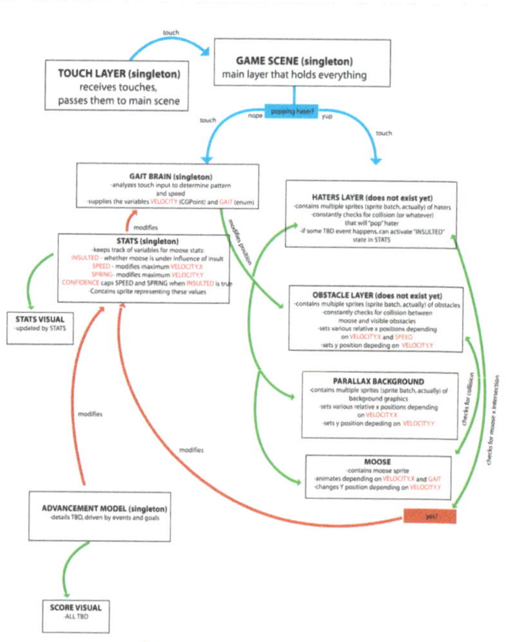

Starfield

Spatial awareness and manipulation in three-dimensions remains a challenge for some students who then become less proficient in science fields like astronomy and engineering. Games are a perfect method to introduce spatial manipulation and lower the barrier to entry in these fields. In our board game prototype **Starfield**, players compete to manipulate cubes with stars on them to form constellations to match their Constellation cards. Starfield aims to improve players' spatial reasoning and 3D mental rotation skills, increasing girls' retention in engineering and related fields.

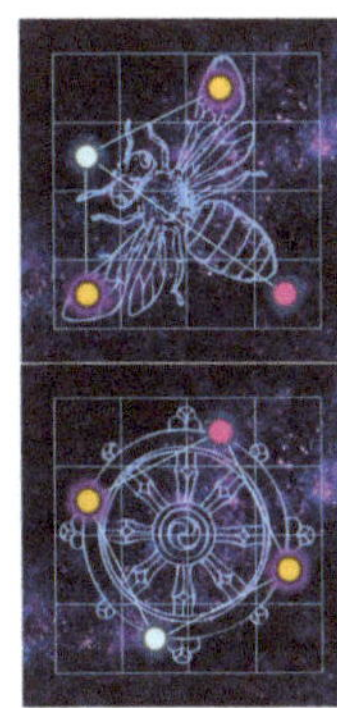

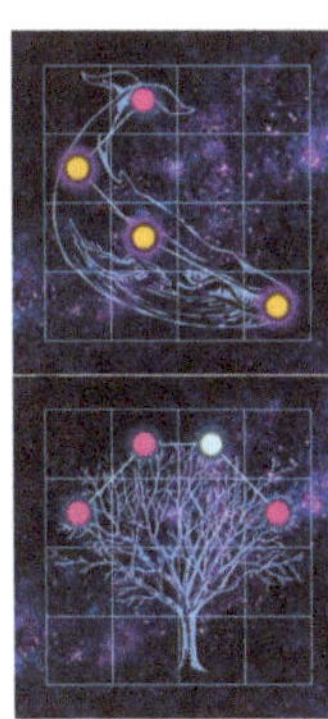

Adventure Capital

In the real world, the best teams build on the strengths of their individual members. Can a game help diversify team-building as well as confront bias? Our prototype **Adventure Capital** set out to accomplish these tasks by allowing players to become the CEO of a company that hires adventurers and sends them to loot treasure on their behalf. To accumulate the most loot, players must recruit the best team by overcoming their biases and hiring people with diverse traits.

Skyline

When students practice their spatial reasoning abilities, they do better in STEM.[31] Could a game that trains players' spatial reasoning abilities cause them to succeed in science classes? **Skyline** is a puzzle game in which players work together to construct buildings so that the skyline of each side of their shared city matches the one shown on the cards. There are no turns — players must effectively communicate with each other to build their skylines. Once all of the sides match their cards, the players beat the level! As they play, players need to consider the impacts that each block placed will have on the other sides of the city, which requires practicing 3D mental rotation spatial skills.

[31] Sorby, S. A., & Baartmans, B. J. (2000). The development and assessment of a course for enhancing the 3-D spatial visualization skills of first year engineering students. *Journal of Engineering Education, 89*(3), 301–07.

Doubtlanders

Stereotype threat remains an entrenched factor that hinders students' ability to succeed in STEM fields and courses. Our board game prototype **Doubtlanders** counters stereotype threat by exposing it and giving kids methods for confronting it. Players take on the role of the citizens of Doubtland and work together to combat the dictatorial rule of the evil Baron Nefarious — who hinders players by using stereotype threat to diminish their skills. **Doubtlanders** also models **growth mindset**, which has been shown to increase retention of women in science classes.

the concept that the only way that we improve (particularly in the sciences) is through practice, and that failing on our first attempts is **not** an indication that we should quit.

Trivance

Can clever riddles lead players to question their assumptions about gender and professions? That was the motivating question as we designed **Trivance**, the game of riddles. In **Trivance**, teams compete to stump each other while balancing objects on their bodies. The asking team reads clues from their Riddle card while the guessing team tries to figure out the answer. For example: "What is Rena? She is known to look down on others. In her work, she often comes across stars. Her job leaves no room for a fear of heights. She needs space in her job. She has made a large step for mankind." (Answer: She's an astronaut!) The game encourages players to overcome implicit bias if they want to win.

ExIsle

One barrier to student success in STEM is the perception that courses and concepts are difficult, intimidating, and don't involve working with other people. Can a game make STEM fields approachable? Our prototype **ExIsle** was designed to do just that. In **ExIsle**, players traverse a natural disaster-wracked, once-thriving island nation and work to collect its lost scientific knowledge — and through that knowledge help its inhabitants and restore its former majesty. Players collect books about STEM, to return to the ancient libraries of **ExIsle** in return for skills to help them in their journeys. **ExIsle** introduces students to STEM fields and concepts, reducing the barrier to understanding them.

WE MAKE GAMES. WE STUDY HO
BELIEVE GAMES ARE CAPABLE OF
CHANGE THE WORLD. W
WE TEACH WITH GA
TRY TO HELP PEOP
WE CREATE. WE
R. GAME DESIGN
buffalo

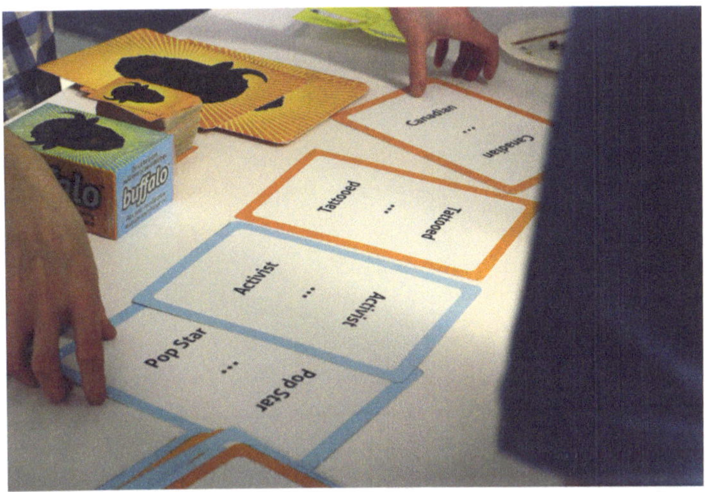
buffalo
Canadian
Tattooed
Activist
Pop Star

got drama?

Considering Impact

The impact of the INTRINSICS project has been significant. Along with 40 research assistant students, we were able to conduct a total of 17 individual studies resulting in 7 published papers and several more under review at leading journals. We included nearly 3000 participants in studies, ranging from high school students, to college students, to the general public, using 12 different "study ready" game prototypes and finished games. In our studies, we harnessed the transformative power of narratives to change norms and improve the climate of STEM classrooms. This makes our research of great practical significance to members of a diverse group of fields and professions, including educators, curriculum specialists, psychologists, designers, and experts in communication and media studies. Our design principles for constructing interactive fictional works encourage empathy, reduce occurrences of bias and inequity, and increase the participation and self-efficacy of underrepresented students in STEM.

The game interventions taken to mass distribution resulted in tens of thousands of copies sold worldwide. It is an amazing moment when people purchase or download their own intervention for personal growth. A workplace training initiative was begun by a collaborator, with the game **Buffalo**, and an associated facilitator's guide made available. The games have been played in locations ranging from college orientations to college classrooms to game development companies such as Zynga.

We've highlighted many key contributions in this book, but several theoretical approaches we've developed stand out to highlight the theoretical novelty and efficacy of this work. From a big-picture perspective, the following discoveries will be useful to anyone engaged in inclusive efforts for more diversity in STEM fields.

First: the Embedded Design model, invented in our EAGER-funded research and manifest in the INTRINSICS project, is a proven design approach for effective interventions. Many interventions utilize a direct, explicit approach to engage people with an issue such as bias or discrimination. They present realistic situations and aim to educate people. This approach does not work well with interactive systems and games, and may limit a game's persuasive impact, because people's psychological defenses activate and effectively "shut out" the message — particularly in areas where people hold unconscious biases, such as in the attitudes and opinions people may hold about women in STEM. In contrast, the Embedded Design approach offers effective, evidence-based strategies for delivering persuasive content using a variety of strategies, such as intermixing (combining "on-topic" and "off-topic" content in order to make the focal message or theme less obvious and more accessible), obfuscating (using game genres or framing devices that direct players' attention or expectations away from the game's true aims), and distancing (employing fiction and metaphor to increase the psychological gap between players' identities and beliefs and the game's characters and content). In this way, people are more open to choose and decide their own path.

Second: we've discovered how to use "aha" moments, the element of surprise, to create a shift in biases against women in STEM. This type of intervention is uncommon as it aims to enlighten the participant by forcing them to address internalized biases and can be effective in the effort to change biases and stereotypes.

Third: we found that narrative matters, but in unexpected and perhaps unintuitive ways. Stories about women facing challenges in STEM contexts can be read by male students as the fault of a lack of preparation rather than the result of infrastructural and unconscious biases. Expressive autobiographical writing can be helpful, but is moderated by personality traits, with self-esteem, public self-consciousness, and the need for cognition playing a significant part in the way women find the activity helpful. Fictional accounts of bias written in the first-person are the best way to immerse readers in the story, and for them to form connections with the characters — they are even more effective than true stories.

Such big-picture discoveries promise to revolutionize the ways that designers of interventions tackle issues of diversity and inclusion in interventions and in games, circumventing psychological defenses and implicit biases and triggering a more receptive mindset for internalizing an intended message, without sacrificing the enjoyment or the engagement of the intervention. Play can be transformative in interventions, and it is important to design such activities with the benefits of what interaction and play truly offer.

Together, our collection of interventions and the research conducted on these interventions forms a robust set of data about novel approaches and interactive designs towards combating the entrenched problem of underrepresentation of women in STEM fields. Even after decades of traditional interventions, women's progress in science and engineering fields lags behind mens'.[32] The INTRINSICS team's inventive design methods coupled with a deep understanding of social psychology, culture, and technology allowed us to create interventions to sustain future generations of STEM talent.

The rich and unique research program, as well as the products of our research made available to the public, continue to encourage healthy dialogue and debate about stereotyping and prejudice. Because the interventions and stories can be widely disseminated as well as experienced multiple times for a vast and diverse user base, we predict the impact of the research will be profound and long-lasting.

[32] https://www.census.gov/prod/2013pubs/acs-24.pdf

WE MAKE GAMES. WE STL
BELIEVE GAMES ARE CAP
GAMES CAN CHANGE THE U
AN ART FORM. WE TEACH L
WITH GAMES. WE TRY TO HE
WE BRAINSTORM. WE CREA
WE ARE TILTFACTOR. GAME

HOW PEOPLE PLAY. WE
OF MORE. WE THINK
. WE THINK GAMES ARE
GAMES. WE SPEAK OUT
EOPLE THROUGH GAMES.
JE RESEARCH. WE PLAY.
IGN FOR SOCIAL CHANGE.

⊞ Accomplishments

From digital interventions and games, to publications in leading journals and presentations at conferences and to the general public, the INTRINSICS project produced tangible contributions to the science of fighting bias in STEM. Below are selected outcomes of the project:

Interventions and Prototypes

Entangled VR puzzle game to allow male students to embody a woman scientist (2019)

The Enchanter point-and-click adventure game to help female STEM students overcome internalized bias and gender rejection sensitivity (2019)

The Investigation pen-and-paper puzzle game to allow students to confront their own biases via an "aha" moment (2017)

Closed Circuit web-based version of **The Investigation** (2018)

I Am More Than website to collect text and visual stories of microaggressions experienced by members of underrepresented groups (2017)

Comics about bias in STEM (2018)

Crowded Dungeon text-based bias situation crowd-sourcing platform (2017)

Dark Secrets of Dartmouth augmented reality campus tour to expose students to Dartmouth role model students who overcame bias to succeed in science (2017)

Dark Secrets of Dartmouth virtual reality version of the campus tour (2018)

Branching narrative stories about Trisha (2017)

Interactive narrative stories about Rosalia and Danielle (2017)

Interactive narrative stories about Trisha (2016)

Publications

Kaufman, G., Flanagan, M. "A Psychologically "Embedded" Approach to Designing Games for Prosocial Causes." Cyberpsychology: Journal of Psychosocial Research on Cyberspace, Special Issue on Videogames, 9(3) 2015, article 5. doi: 10.5817/CP2015-3-5

Freedman, G., & Flanagan, M. (2017). "From dictators to avatars: Furthering social and personality psychology through game methods." Social and Personality Psychology Compass, e12368. doi: 10.1111/spc3.12368

Green, M. C., Kaufman, G., Flanagan, M., & Fitzgerald, K. (2017). "Self-esteem and public self-consciousness moderate the emotional impact of expressive writing about experiences with bias." Personality and Individual Differences.

Freedman, G., Green, M. C., Flanagan, M., Fitzgerald, K., & Kaufman, G., (2018). "The effect of gender on attributions for women's anxiety and doubt in a science narrative." Psychology of Women Quarterly.

Freedman, G., Seidman, M., Flanagan, M., Kaufman, G., & Green, M. C. (2018). "Updating a classic: A new generation of vignette experiments involving iterative decision-making." Advances in Methods and Practices in Psychological Science. https://doi.org/10.1016/j.jesp.2018.03.014

Freedman, G., Seidman, M., Flanagan, M., Kaufman, G., & Green, M. C. (2018). "The impact of an "aha" moment on gender biases: Limited evidence for the efficacy of a game intervention that challenges gender assumptions." Journal of Experimental Social Psychology.

Freedman, G., Green, M. C., Flanagan, M., & Kaufman, G. (2019). "Obituaries can popularize science and health:

Stephen Hawking and interest in cosmology and amyotrophic lateral sclerosis." Psychology of Popular Media Culture. Advance online publication.

Freedman, G., Flanagan, M., Seidman, M. (Upcoming). Using a game intervention to decrease self-doubt among female undergraduate STEM students.

Freedman, G., Green, M. C., Seidman, M., Flanagan, M. (Upcoming). The Effect of Playing a Female Physicist in Virtual Reality on Men's Gender Biases.

General Public Presentations

Research at Dartmouth, Trustees of Dartmouth College Meeting, March 1, 2019

Centennial Circle Forum. April 15, 2016

The Games People Play (The Science of Bias at Salt Hill Pub) Sept, 2017

Tiltfactor Laboratory Open House. August 27, 2017

Class visits about bias. Winter and Spring 2018

Tiltfactor Department Open House for the public and prospective students. July 14, 2018

Tiltfactor Department Open House for the public and prospective students. September 7, 2018

Q&A Sessions on Games and Science, Hanover High School Chemistry and Engineering classes. June 2018

Sessions at Hanover High School. March 22 2018

Career awareness day, Lebanon New Hampshire. March 24, 2018

Talk and Q&A on Games and Science, Hartford High School. November 13, 2018 Talk and Q&A on Games and Science, Second Start school. February 15 2018

Dartmouth Great Issues Scholars. Feb 27 2018

Dartmouth: Top of the Hop Community sampling of interventions. May 4th 2018

Dartmouth: Top of the Hop Community sampling of interventions. January 20 2018

Interview with Mary Flanagan on New Hampshire Public Radio. May 8 2018

Scholarly Presentations

Green, M. C., Kaufman, G., & Flanagan, M. (2015). Self-esteem and public self-consciousness moderate the emotional impact of expressive writing about experiences with bias. Poster presented at the International Communication Association annual meeting. Fukuoka, Japan.

Green, M. C., Freedman, G., Kaufman, G., Fitzgerald, K., & Flanagan, M. (2017). Interpretations of a science bias narrative vary by gender. Society for Personality and Social Psychology. San Antonio

Kaufman, G & Green, M. C. (2015) "Using Stories to Increase Understanding of Gender Bias and Stereotype Threat in STEM," NSF ADVANCE/GSE Program Workshop in Baltimore, Maryland

Freedman, G., Seidman, M., Flanagan, M., Green, M. C., Kaufman, G. (2018)"Decreasing Self-Doubt Among Female Undergraduate STEM Students with a Digital Game," NCA 104th Annual Convention Nov 8-11 Salt Lake City

⊞ About the Author

Dr. Mary Flanagan[33] is a scholar, artist, futurist, and designer whose games, installations, poetry, and essays forge a unique vision of technology, pop culture, and the avant-garde. With five scholarly books, more than fifty essays and chapters, and a collection of poetry to her credit, Dr. Flanagan's writing has also appeared in Salon, USA Today, the San Francisco Chronicle, Gamasutra, and The Daily Beast. Her internationally recognized artwork ranges from game-inspired systems to computer viruses, embodied interfaces to interactive texts. Her artwork has been exhibited at museums around the world such as: The Whitney Museum, The Guggenheim, Tate Britain, and museums in Germany, Spain, New Zealand, South Korea, and Australia.

Dr. Flanagan is the recipient of the American Council of Learned Societies Digital Innovation Fellowship, the Brown Foundation Fellowship, the MacDowell Colony Fellowship, the Bogliasco Fellowship, and a John Paul Getty Museum Scholar. She was Senior Scholar in Residence at the Cornell Society for the Humanities, a Distinguished Visiting Scholar at the Jackman Humanities Institute of the University of Toronto, and a Distinguished Visiting Artist at the Georgia Institute of Technology. In 2016, she was honored as a 'Vanguard' from Games for Change and received an Honoris Causa in Design from the Illinois Institute of Technology. Dr. Flanagan has served on the White House Office of Science and Technology Policy (OSTP) Academic Consortium on Games for Impact, and her work has been supported by commissions and grants including The British Arts Council, the National Science Foundation, the National Institute of Justice, the National Endowment for the Humanities, and the Institute of Museum and Library Services.

Dr. Flanagan holds a B.A. from the University of Wisconsin, Milwaukee, a M.F.A. from the University of Iowa, and a Ph.D. from Central Saint Martins College of Art and Design at the University of the Arts, London. She teaches at Dartmouth College, where she serves as the Sherman Fairchild Distinguished Professor of Digital Humanities.

[33] www.maryflanagan.com

 The Lab

Dr. Flanagan's lab Tiltfactor occupies a loft design studio in the Black Family Visual Arts Center at Dartmouth College, where the team fuses a creative approach to art, technology, and innovation. The lab's personality is matched by its playful, modern space with a comprehensive collection of game consoles, analog and digital game libraries, video conferencing stations, and brainstorming, design and prototyping areas.

The Tiltfactor lab is indebted to its staff, which includes game designers, researchers, visual artists, graphic designers, information architects and programmers, and undergraduate and postgraduate students. The team's diverse academic and personal backgrounds enable the lab to design games that forge new styles of play. Research in the lab is conducted across design science, learning, psychology, computer science, information science, systems design/engineering, and media studies.

246 Black Family Visual Arts Center
22 Lebanon Street
Dartmouth College
Hanover, New Hampshire 03755

(603) 646-1007
@tiltfactor
www.tiltfactor.org
contact@tiltfactor.org

This research has been supported by NSF grants:
#HRD-1137483
#DRL-1420036